Colonial and Early American Fashions

Tom Tierney

DOVER PUBLICATIONS, INC.
Mineola, New York

INTRODUCTION

The age of European colonialism began in 1492 with the landing of Europeans in the region that we know today as the Americas. Portugal created colonies in South America; Spain established its presence primarily in Mexico, Florida, and Southern California.

In 1624, the Dutch West India Company founded New Amsterdam, a settlement that encompassed the land that is now known as Manhattan. It ran along the Hudson River, north to Albany. With the best harbor in North America, New Amsterdam attracted settlers from England, France, Scandinavia, Ireland, and Germany. The English took possession of New Amsterdam in 1674, changing the name to New York.

Between 1609 and 1632, English settlers arrived in the West Indies to trade in sugar, logging, and slavery. Pirates also established colonies there. The original American colonies, Virginia (1602), Plymouth (1620), and Massachusetts Bay (1630), were first populated by religious dissenters. Carolina colonies were founded in 1630; Georgia, the last of the original 13 colonies, was established in 1732. The English were later joined by the French, Germans, Scots, Irish, Danes, and Swiss. By 1763, several cities had developed, including New York, Boston, Philadelphia, Baltimore, and Charleston.

The French established New France in Canada in 1663, using it as a base from which to explore the Mississippi River. Claiming the land now known as Louisiana, in 1718 they established the city of New Orleans.

One of North America's most profitable commodities was beaver pelt for which there seemed to be an insatiable demand in Europe. By the 1700s, however, the beaver was nearly extinct in New York. In search of fresh populations, trappers moved westward.

When the English took possession of New Amsterdam and its environs, the wealthy Dutch inhabitants were influenced by English fashions, ushering in the beginning of a unique American colonial look which would eventually borrow from many European sources. By 1700, the greatest influence in colonial fashion was England, with most colonials, from Massachusetts to Virginia, ordering clothing, fabrics, pattern books, and furnishings from the "mother country."

Note: Although the colors indicated in the following descriptions are based on the original reference materials, feel free to create your own color schemes. Happy coloring!

Bibliographical Note

Colonial and Early American Fashions is a new work, first published by
Dover Publications, Inc., in 1999.

International Standard Book Number

ISBN-13: 978-0-486-40364-9
ISBN-10: 0-486-40364-5

Manufactured in the United States by Courier Corporation
40364509   2014
www.doverpublications.com

Pirates (1620–50)

When not sailing, pirates enjoyed dressing in the finery that they looted from ships. Here, a pirate presents a woman with a trunkful of stylish plunder. The man wears a red jupe, or jacket, with slashed sleeves and red, full cut breeches, known as Spanish slops. Multicolor ribbons decorate the edges of his jacket and sash. He wears a white frilled shirt with a lace-edged fall at his neck. His accessories include yellow hose, black shoes with red heels and bows, and a black hat with ostrich plumes. The woman wears a rose silk gown with ecru lace inserts, a white chemise, and a white lingerie cap.

Pirates (1640)

Anne Bonney and Mary Read were notorious Carolina pirates. Working in men's sailor clothing, they are shown here wearing white shirts over colored corsets, and men's tan or blue cotton pantaloons. One female pirate wears a navy blue coat and black felt hat; the other wears a dark red jacket with a gray felt hat.

Puritans (1620)

Although black was the prevalent color, Puritans also wore garments that were brown, maroon, dark blue, dark green, violet, gray, and tan. Puritan women often chose scarlet for cloaks, petticoats, and hoods. Their shoes and hats were brown or black. Children were often dressed in colors.

Maryland Settlers (1630)

The woman wears a bodice and gown of blue-violet wool with an underskirt of yellow brocaded silk. Her collar, called a falling band, is edged with eyelet embroidery. She holds a white apron which she will tuck and tie under her bodice. On her shoes, she wears brightly colored ribbon rosettes. The man, carrying a musket and musket vest, wears a natural leather jerkin over a white shirt, and dark slops with green wool stockings.

Dutch Settlers Skating on the Hudson River (1630)

The man wears a split leather, fur-lined sheepskin coat topped by a dark wool shawl. He also wears a split leather hood and cap, dark brown slops with matching ribbon, red hose, brown leather shoes with red heels, and wooden skates with leather ties. The woman wears a deep purple wool gown over a red lace-edged petticoat, a fur collar, and a purple hood. She carries a red wool muff and wears brown leather shoes with red rosettes. The stiffened silk mask protects her face from the wind.

7

Dutch Ladies of New Amsterdam (1630)

The woman on the left wears a tobacco brown bodice, sleeves, and skirt over a lavender, white lace-edged underskirt. Her white bertha (a deep, cape-like collar), is edged in lace with matching sleeve cuffs. Covering her head is a brown hooded chaperon. She carries a fox muff; on her feet are yellow leather shoes. The woman on the right wears a soft green satin gown with a white bertha, a black chaperon, and a black fur muff.

Hudson River Dutch Patroons, or Landholders (1630)

The woman wears a pastel brocaded silk bodice and a full sleeved-peplum. Her white bertha with a dropped neckline is trimmed with lace and eyelet embroidery. She wears a matching satin skirt and bodice. A hand mirror hangs from her waist. The man wears a dark gray taffeta doublet, a dark gray wool cloak, and breeches trimmed with black ribbons. His white shirt shows through the slashed sleeves of his doublet. His laced-edged white fall, or collar, matches his cuffs. He wears a black felt hat and black shoes with dark gray stockings.

Tom Tierney

Danish Colonists from Pennsylvania (1650)

The man wears a gray wool cape, an olive green doublet, and brown slops, or breeches. His accessories include a brown fur hat, gray hose, and brown leather shoes. The bodice of the woman's gown is striped in blue-gray and white; her skirt is also blue-gray. Her white muslin apron is trimmed with multicolored embroidery. She wears a brown wool cape, a white linen cap, and brown leather shoes.

Dutch Lady and Merchant-Exporter from New Amsterdam (1650)

She wears a blue silk gown trimmed with white lace. Her ribbon belt and baldric (a diagonal sash), are pale blue; her broad collar and fall are white linen with eyelet embroidery. She wears a white lace cap. The man's leather jerkin is rust brown with shoulder wings. His broad collar lies flat in the front, and flips up in the back.

He wears separate sleeves which have small slashings that reveal his white shirt. At his neck is a white ruff, and at his wrists are white cuffs. His trousers are black or dark gray with dark green silk side stripes ending in rosettes. He wears a red sash belt, red hose, brown shoes, a gray felt hat, and gloves.

11

Mother and Child, English Commonwealth (1650)

The girl wears an apple green satin gown. Her collar, her sleeves, and her apron are edged with white lace. Her white cap is topped with a pink satin bow; she carries a pink rose. Her mother wears a rose satin gown with con- trasting white cuffs, apron, and gloves. Her bodice and skirt match. Around her shoulders is a black shawl, and she wears a black wool, hooded chaperon. She carries a clipped black ostrich fan.

New Amsterdam Townspeople (1650)

The man's gray felt hat matches the lining, lapels, and cuffs of his black wool coat. His waistcoat, also wool, is rust-colored with a pale blue sash. He wears steel blue breeches, gray hose, and black shoes with blue ribbon ties. The townswoman wears a tan bodice and sleeves, both trimmed with ecru embroidery. She has a white falling collar and white cap. Her light blue skirt, trimmed with ecru embroidery, covers a scarlet wool petticoat. She wears black leather shoes. They are supported by brown leather and wood pattens on iron rings to protect them from mud.

Wealthy Dutch Patroon Couple (1660)

This man, a wealthy landowner, wears a short, gold satin doublet with slashed sleeves that show his white linen shirt. At his neck is a large, turned-down collar. He wears black wool knee-length breeches edged with red and white rolled ribbon. There are red ribbon loops at the waist and hem. His black cape is held in place by a baldric, or diagonal sash. He wears blue stockings, white boot hose, and black shoes with red ties. The woman's satin gown, pale orchid, is appliquéd with ecru lace. At her neck, she wears a white bertha. Her cuffs are white.

Dutch Couple in Formal Dress (1670)

The man's medium blue wool coat, trimmed with gold braid, is lined in gold satin. His full breeches are matching blue. He also wears a gold waistcoat, a blue velvet hat with white ostrich plumes, a white fall, and white boot hose. He has yellow leather gloves, and brown boots with red heels. (At this period, red heels were very popular on men's boots.) The woman's gown has a green velvet bodice, and short, slashed sleeves over her white chemise. Her lavender petticoat matches the ribbon trim and bows.

A Lady of New Amsterdam (1675)

When the English took over New Amsterdam, English fashions became the mode. This lady wears a wine-colored satin gown in the style of the English Restoration. It has a deep shoulder bertha in ecru, to match the exposed chemise sleeve. The skirt, parted at the front, reveals a blue underskirt over an ecru petticoat.

French Immigrant Farmers (1680–1700)

The man wears a pumpkin colored justaucorps, or coat, over a white shirt and brown wide-legged petticoat breeches. His white fall has pink and blue ribbon ties which match the ribbons on his breeches. He carries a brown felt hat, and wears brown shoes. The woman's gown has a medium blue bodice with yellow trim. She wears a white chemise and ruff. Her blue skirt, tucked up in the French style, matches her petticoat. On her feet are brown leather shoes.

Colonial Lady from North America (1660–1685)

During the English Restoration period (1660–1689) styles were eagerly copied by colonial residents. This lady wears a brocaded silk gown in soft red with a white satin stomacher (an article of clothing that was worn over the breast), and underskirt. It has puffed sleeves edged with red fringe. The dropped neckline has a flounce of white lace. The chemise sleeves and underskirt are also trimmed in white lace. The ribbons on her stomacher are blue velvet, as are the ribbons holding back the skirt. Her hair is arranged over a wire frame.

A Wealthy American Merchant Couple (1685–1700)

The woman wears a Restoration style gown of rose velvet with long slashed sleeves. Her gray satin underskirt is caught up to one side; her white chemise is visible at the neck and cuffs. Yellow silk bow knots adorn her hair and gown. The man's costume includes a short doublet with slashed sleeves which he wears over a white lawn shirt with a lace-edged, pleated falling band. His petticoat breeches, with ribbon loops called cannons, match his doublet. He wears lace-edged boot hose and brown leather boots which have fashionable red heels.

A Conservative Lady (1685–1700)

Her day gown, of dark colored cloth, has an open front with slashed, elbow-length sleeves. Her silk stomacher and petticoat are a muted color. She wears a white lawn collar. Her chemise and hood match her gown.

An English Colonist (1710–1725)

When the French influenced the court fashions in England, their impact was felt by people in the colonies, too. This lady wears an iridescent pink and green striped satin gown in the French style, with a gray silk stomacher. Her chemise is white lawn. Around her neck she wears a twisted lace scarf and over her shoulders is a black silk mantilla with a ruched (or gathered) edge. Accessories include a white lawn cap, white shoes, and white kid gloves.

Two Ladies Dressed in the French Style (1720–1730)

The woman on the left wears a Watteau gown in pastel satin with a silk underskirt and laced bodice in the same color. The gown has pagoda sleeves, which flare at the elbow. She has natural hair and a white lingerie cap. The woman on the right wears a pale-colored taffeta gown with a matching gimp-edged (or braided) underskirt. The gown has a white lingerie neck and sleeve ruffles. She wears embroidered yellow-toned shoes, and green hose. Her powdered hair is covered by a white lingerie cap trimmed with yellow satin ribbons.

An American Lady (1725–1740)

This lady wears a Watteau gown of boldly printed silk. The fabric has a dark green ground with a multicolored floral design. She wears a yellow satin petticoat and carries a matching fan. She has turned down the lappets of her white lawn lingerie cap.

An English Colonial Merchant Couple (1725)

By the first quarter of the 18th century, American colonial fashions were predominately influenced by the English. Over her chemise, this woman wears a wine-colored day dress with short sleeves. A white fichu (or ruffled fabric) is draped over her bosom. Worn over oval pocket hoops, the dress has a white stomacher. The woman wears white gloves; a white kerchief adorns her head. The man wears a blue coat with boot cuffed sleeves, narrow blue breeches, and a gold brocade waistcoat. His white shirt has a white fall and black cravat. Accessories include a black hat with gold braid, black shoes, and sword. His hair is powdered.

Swiss-Protestant Immigrants in Georgia (1730–1740)

The woman, carrying a red, green, and white striped bag, wears a maroon jacket trimmed with a band of black satin embroidered with pink. Her coral bodice overlaps a pale blue apron and a black skirt with pink trim. She wears coral hose, and black shoes with maroon vamps. She also wears a white chemise, a straw hat, and a black ribbon around her neck . The man wears a white linen justaucorps (a close fitting coat), white breeches, white hose, and brown shoes. His waistcoat is dark red, and he wears a white cap under his felt hat.

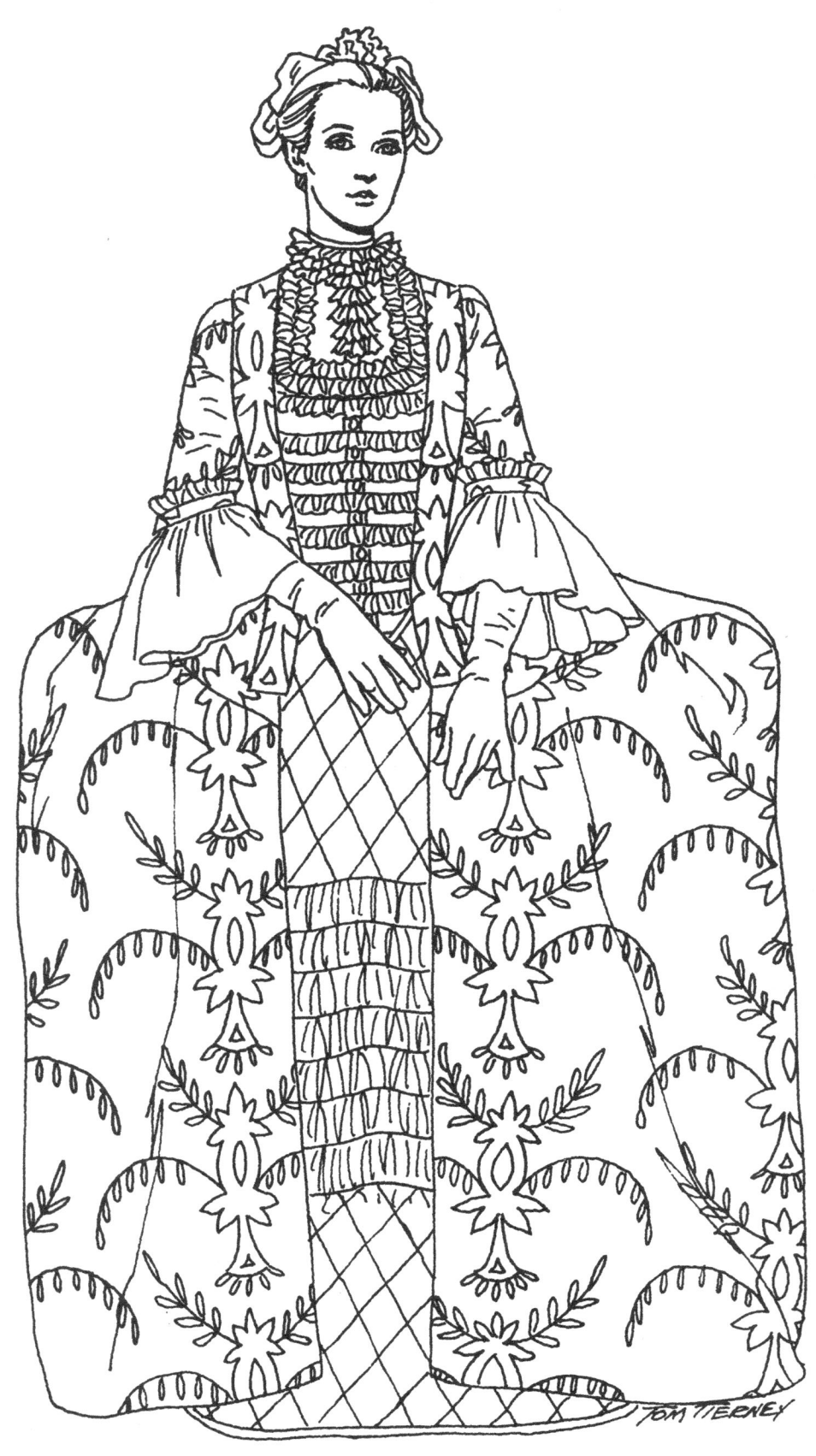

A Colonial Lady (1745)

She wears wide, double pannier hoops. Her open, lapelled robe is pink-on-rose satin brocade. Her rose silk bodice has rows of ruffles, and her white chemise shows ruffles at the sleeve. She wears a gray satin, quilted, petticoat and pink gloves.

American Colonial Girl (1730–40)

This girl wears a printed cotton dress. It has a blue-green background with cream, orange, and yellow flowers. The bodice is laced with yellow ribbon. She wears a white fichu, and a chemise. There is a cap under her straw hat. She wears gray stockings, black shoes, and carries a black bag.

A Farm Girl in Her Best Dress (1725–1735)

Her cotton print dress has orange flowers and green leaves on a yellow ground. It is covered with a white fichu and white apron. Because she wears no stomacher, this girl's white chemise is visible under the lacing. Her white lawn cap sits at the back of her head, the front turned back to form lappets. She wears brown shoes.

Colonial Lady in a Formal Gown (1740–1750)

Her blue silk gown has robings (or shoulder straps), and pleated sleeve cuffs of pink-on-blue brocade. Her stomacher, blouse, and lace frills are ecru. The white ruffles around her neck are called "Betsies," after Queen Elizabeth I. She wears a white cap, called a "pinner" because the side lappets could be pinned up. Her pink gloves are satin, a popular fabric because it looked lavish and could be spot cleaned with relative ease.

Two Scottish Immigrants (1745)

England passed the Dress Act in 1747, making it illegal to wear Highland clothes. Offenders could be deported to the colonies for seven years. The man pictured here wears a coat, breeches, hose, and a cape in red and black plaid. His balderic, or sash, is black. On his feet are black shoes with silver buckles. Additional accessories include a dagger, a sword sheath, and a purse. The woman wears a blue wrap-over gown, sans bodice, over a white chemise which shows at the neckline and sleeves. She wears a long plaid scarf.

A Quaker Woman from Pennsylvania (1750–1770)

Quaker women preferred the fabric of their clothing to be soft, muted tones. This Quaker woman wears a lavender-gray cotton dress with long fitted sleeves, a white lawn fichu and a white cap. Her apron is pale green lawn.

A Shop Girl or Maid (1750–60)

The English emptied their prisons of many petty criminals by shipping them to the American colonies as bonded workers. Their clothing was often fashioned from previously worn garments which had been stripped of all frills and furbelows. This woman is wearing a white muslin mob-cap and fichu. Her white muslin apron covers a striped cotton sacque and a dark wool skirt. In place of hoops, she is wearing several petticoats. On her feet are knitted wool stockings, and leather pattens with wooden soles.

Anglo-American Colonists Dancing (1750–1765)

The woman is wearing a gown of medium-toned silk and a white lawn cap, both trimmed with ecru lace trim. Her shoes are brocaded silk. The man wears a long, flared, dark justaucorps, white hose, and black shoes. His powdered wig is held back with a black silk tie.

Townspeople, Laborers or Artisans (1720–1770)

The man, with bobbed, natural hair, wears a light brown wool coat and darker breeches. His waistcoat is gray worsted; his shirt is unbleached muslin. On his feet are gray wool stockings and brown leather shoes. The woman's dress is sage green-and-tan striped. She wears a white cotton cap, a white cotton apron, and a white blouse.

Colonial Winter Outerwear (1750–1770)

The woman wears a dark wool, hooded cloak trimmed with fur and dark velvet ribbons. It covers a dark dress and dark gloves. The man wears a fawn colored riding coat with a triple layered shoulder cape. His frock coat is dark wool; his breeches are tan. He wears a black felt hat and black leather riding boots.

An Indentured Maid Servant or Country Girl (1760–1770)

She wears a lilac and maroon striped cotton dress with a white fichu and chemise. Her turquoise blue underskirt is striped with yellow. Her apron and muslin cap are white; on her feet are gray hose and calfskin shoes.

Virginia Settlers (1760–70)

The man's justaucorps is dark wool with brass buttons. His waistcoat is a light color, and his breeches are tan. He wears white stockings and black shoes. The young woman wears a floral silk gown with a solid color, quilted petticoat. Her mob cap, fichu, and stomacher are white; her bows and shoes are colored silk.

A Colonial Merchant and his Family (1760–1770)

The merchant's suit is dark blue silk with a tan waistcoat. His stockings, shirt and fall are white. The young boy wears a rust-colored jacket and skirt (boys wore skirts until about the age of 5), with a white shirt. The young girl wears a rose-colored silk gown with a white apron, blouse, and sleeves. Their mother is dressed in a dark green silk gown with a white petticoat, a white stomacher, and a white cap. Her fichu is dark lace.

A Colonial Gentleman Farming Couple (1760)

The lady's silk gown has pink and green roses on a coral background. She wears a white-on-white lawn apron, the top styled as a fichu. Under her straw hat, which is trimmed with a pink ribbon, she wears a white lace cap.

The man wears a green silk coat. His waistcoat and breeches are tan silk; both have gold buttons and trim. His hair is powdered.

An English Officer and a Colonial Lady (1760)

The officer's white wool coat is trimmed with gold braid. The cuffs have red silk bands. His waistcoat and breeches are gold colored silk; the waistcoat has gold braid trim. The sash is also gold fabric. The lady's pale yellow silk gown has a pink rose trellis pattern. She wears a white fichu and stomacher with a yellow bow. There is white lace trim at edge of the fichu, sleeves, and skirt. Her straw milk maid's hat is trimmed with pink ribbon.

A Colonial Couple (1750–1775)

The gentleman is lacing the woman's pastel-colored corset. She wears an unbleached muslin petticoat over an oval hoop constructed of cane. Tied around her waist is an embroidered pocket, which she can reach through a slit in her gown. She wears a white chemise and cap.

The man wears a brocaded satin banyan (or loose wrap), and a turban. Men often kept their heads shaved to facilitate wearing a wig, or a turban, which provided warmth. His shirt is white muslin and his breeches are a light color.

A Gentleman and Lady (1770)

The gentleman with a quizzing glass wears an amber satin coat and breeches; his waistcoat is cream satin. Both waistcoat and coat are trimmed in gold braid. His hair is powdered. The lady's silk gown has an eggshell blue background printed with pink and yellow flowers. The white scarf at her neck is fastened by a jeweled brooch. The underskirt and frills are made from finely pleated ecru mull. Over her powdered hair, she wears a sheer cap with ecru frills.

A Colonial Lady in Formal Dress (1770)

Her open gown is pearl gray satin. Multicolored embroidery decorates the skirt panels and the bottom of the matching underskirt. The sleeve flounces are white sheer; the bows on the sleeves and at the bosom are colored silk. Her hair is powdered white or gray; on her head she wears a festoon of lace.

Hats and Hair Styles (1650 to 1695)

a. Beaver hat, lingerie cap, and falling band (1650). **b.** Felt hat with white lawn band (1650). **c.** Felt hat, white linen cap and falling band (1650). **d.** Powdered wig, twisted cravat with lace ends (1680). **e.** Curls dressed over a wire frame (1680). **f.** Beaver hat, ostrich plumes, black wig, lace cravat (1670). **g.** Beaver hat, ribbon loops, and ostrich plume (1685). **h.** Tricorne with uncurled ostrich plume, lace cravat, and powdered wig (1695). **i.** Wig, falling band, and band strings (1680). **j.** Dark wig with falling band (1685).

Hats and Hair Styles (1728 to 1770)

a. Lace edged lingerie cap, ribbon bow (1731). **b.** Straw hat, natural hair (1735). **c.** Lingerie cap, lace edging, powdered hair, artificial flowers (1731). **d.** Bag wig, pigeon's wings side curls (1728). **e.** Powdered hair and ostrich plumes for formal dress (1771). **f.** Lace hood with striped ribbon (1750). **g.** Colored silk kerchief over powdered wig (1750). **h.** Natural hair (1764). **i.** Velvet tricorne hat with gold braid, jeweled loop button, powdered hair, and lace collarette (1745). **j.** Informal beaver hat, natural hair, black ribbon tie (1750). **k.** Powdered hair (1770). **l.** Short hair style, natural color (1745). **m.** Powdered hair with pearls (1755). **n.** Straw hat over lace cap (1770). **o.** Natural hair worn in a French twist (1755). **p.** Natural hair, fur collar (1765).

Footwear (1600 to 1690)

a. Man's shoe, shoe rose, attached patten (1600). **b.** Man's shoe, large shoe rose with jeweled center (1630). **c.** Man's white leather shoe, with red heel, shoe rose, punched design, (1620). **d.** Lady's shoe, striped silk, white heel (1640). **e.** Man's leather boot with red heel and spur leather on vamp (1620). **f.** Lady's embroidered leather slipper (1620). **g.** Lady's kid shoe with satin bow (1650). **h.** Man's shoe with shoe rose, slip on patten (1630). **i.** Lady's embroidered silk shoe (1680). **j.** Lady's stitched leather shoe (1640). **k.** Man's lace-edged boot hose with red heel and sole, bucket top, and spur leather (1640). **l.** Man's tongued shoe with silk ties, and red heels, (1640). **m.** Man's bucket top boot with spur leather, (1690). **n.** Lady's shoe with lace ruffle (1690). **o.** Man's shoe, red heel, buckled (1690).

Footwear (1700 to 1760)

a. Lady's embroidered shoe (1700). **b.** Lady's pantoffle, or mule (1710). **c.** Man's black shoe, red tongue and heel (1700). **d.** Man's shoe, red heel (1700). **e.** Lady's shoe, embroidered white kid, jeweled buckle (1730). **f.** Lady's shoe, kid and black velvet, attached clog (1700). **g.** Man's shoe, black leather, red heel, jeweled buckle (1730). **h.** Fitted buskin, boot hose frill (1700). **i.** Jack boot (1700). **j.** Man's shoe, windmill wing ties (1720).

k. Man's leather mule, or slipper (1750). **l.** Man's leather spatterdashes (1710). **m.** Lady's embroidered shoe (1745). **n.** Lady's tongued shoe (1755). **o.** Lady's tongued shoe, embroidered (1755). **p.** Lady's kid leather shoe (1740). **q.** Lady's kid leather shoe (1760). **r.** Man's shoe, black leather, jeweled buckle (1740). **s.** Lady's slipper, gold satin with silk flowers (1760).